The Pocket Book of
KINDNESS

The Pocket Book of
KINDNESS

Inspirational thoughts on goodness and generosity

SIRIUS

SIRIUS

This edition published in 2018 by Sirius Publishing, a division of
Arcturus Publishing Limited,
26/27 Bickels Yard, 151–153 Bermondsey Street,
London SE1 3HA

ISBN: 978-1-78888-326-9
AD006310UK

Printed in China

Contents

Introduction

Lady Macbeth described it as "milk"- a pallid, insipid sentiment that weakens her husband's resolve. Franklin D. Roosevelt disagreed: "Human kindness has never weakened the stamina or softened the fibre of a free people", he proclaimed.

Yet, amid the blizzard of accounts of cruelty that blows out daily from our televisions and radios, rarely are we granted the respite of a tale of kindness to lighten the heart. Notable exceptions stand out: Mother Teresa, Florence Nightingale, Androcles, Winnie the Pooh. . . but they are few and far between. It seems that cruelty is more compelling.

The truth is that simple acts of kindness happen all the time. It is fundamental to our nature to be kind, generous, benevolent, altruistic, philanthropic, empathetic, sympathetic and caring. Kindness is, indeed, a sign of strength, for it comes from a position of confidence and is given without fear of the consequences. As Mahatma Gandhi said, "The simplest acts of kindness are by far more powerful than a thousand heads bowing in prayer."

The word kindness is linked to kin, kindred and the German *kinder*, meaning children. It implies oneness, unity and nurture - the sense that we are all in this together. As this book reveals, amid all the cruelty, kindness is never far from the minds of people, nor from their deeds.

WHAT IS KINDNESS?

Kindness is
the language which the
deaf can hear and the
blind can see.

Mark Twain

Kindness is the sunshine
in which virtue grows.

Robert Green Ingersoll

Sweet mercy is nobility's true badge.

William Shakespeare

Amnesty is as good for those who give it as for those who receive it. It has the admirable quality of bestowing mercy on both sides.

Victor Hugo

Pity may represent little more than the impersonal concern which prompts the mailing of a check, but true sympathy is the personal concern which demands the giving of one's soul.

Martin Luther King, Jr.

13

Kindness is ever the begetter of kindness.

Sophocles

Kindness is loving people more than they deserve.

Joseph Joubert

Life is mostly froth and bubble,
Two things stand like stone
Kindness in another's trouble,
Courage in your own.

Adam Lindsay Gordon

A kind heart is a
fountain of gladness,
making everything
in its vicinity freshen
into smiles.

Washington Irving

16

A warm smile is the universal language of kindness.

William Arthur Ward

Any mind that is capable
of real sorrow is capable
of good.

Harriet Beecher Stowe

Care is a state in
which something does
matter; it is the source
of human tenderness.

Rollo May

Character is made of duty
and love and sympathy,
and, above all, of living
and working for others.

Robert Green Ingersoll

Compassion brings us to a stop, and for a moment we rise above ourselves.

Mason Cooley

21

Compassion is a call,
a demand of nature,
to relieve the unhappy as
hunger is a natural call
for food.

Joseph Butler

Compassion is not weakness, and concern for the unfortunate is not socialism.

Hubert H. Humphrey

Compassion is sometimes the fatal capacity for feeling what it is like to live inside somebody else's skin. It is the knowledge that there can never really be any peace and joy for me until there is peace and joy finally for you too.

Frederick Buechner

Compassion is the antitoxin of the soul: where there is compassion even the most poisonous impulses remain relatively harmless.

Eric Hoffer

Compassion is the basis of morality.

Arthur Schopenhauer

Empathy is the faculty to resonate with the feelings of others. When we meet someone who is joyful, we smile. When we witness someone in pain, we suffer in resonance with his or her suffering.

Matthieu Ricard

For me, forgiveness and compassion are always linked: how do we hold people accountable for wrongdoing and yet at the same time remain in touch with their humanity enough to believe in their capacity to be transformed?

bell hooks

Generosity during life is a very different thing from generosity in the hour of death; one proceeds from genuine liberality and benevolence, the other from pride or fear.

Horace Mann

Generosity is giving more
than you can, and pride is
taking less than you need.

Kahlil Gibran

Generosity is not giving me that which I need more than you do, but it is giving me that which you need more than I do.

Kahlil Gibran

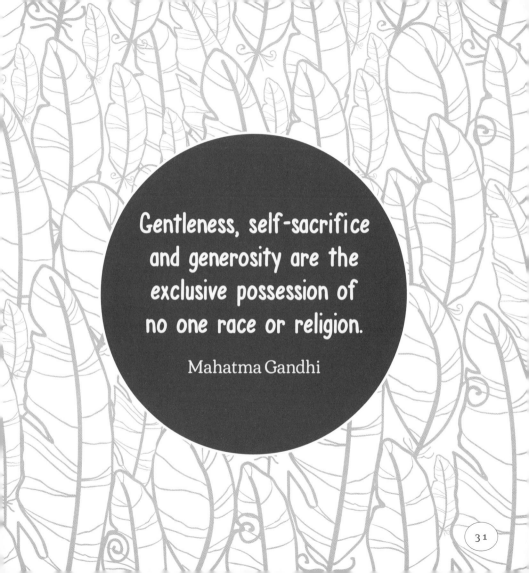

Gentleness, self-sacrifice
and generosity are the
exclusive possession of
no one race or religion.

Mahatma Gandhi

Harshness and
unkindness are relative.
The appearance of them
may be the fruits of the
greatest kindness.

William Godwin

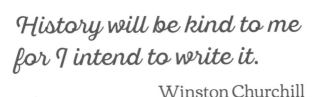

History will be kind to me for I intend to write it.

Winston Churchill

Human it is to have compassion on the unhappy.

Giovanni Boccaccio

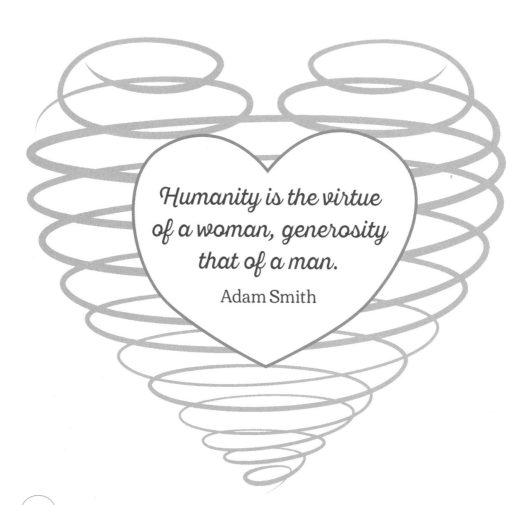

Humanity is the virtue
of a woman, generosity
that of a man.

Adam Smith

I slept and I dreamed that life is all joy.
I woke and I saw that life is all service. I
served and I saw that service is joy.

Kahlil Gibran

It is kindness
to immediately
refuse what you
intend to deny.

Publilius Syrus

Kindness in ourselves
is the honey that blunts the
sting of unkindness
in another.

Walter Savage Landor

Kindness is a passport
that opens doors and fashions
friends. It softens hearts and
molds relationships that
can last lifetimes.

Joseph B. Wirthlin

Kindness is an everyday byproduct of all the great virtues.

Krista Tippett

Kindness is not about instant gratification. More often, it's akin to a low-risk investment that appreciates steadily over time.

Josh Radnor

Kindness is the essence of greatness and the fundamental characteristic of the noblest men and women I have known.

Joseph B. Wirthlin

Kindness is the greatest
beauty that you can have.

Andie MacDowell

**Kindness, I've
discovered, is
everything in life.**

Isaac Bashevis Singer

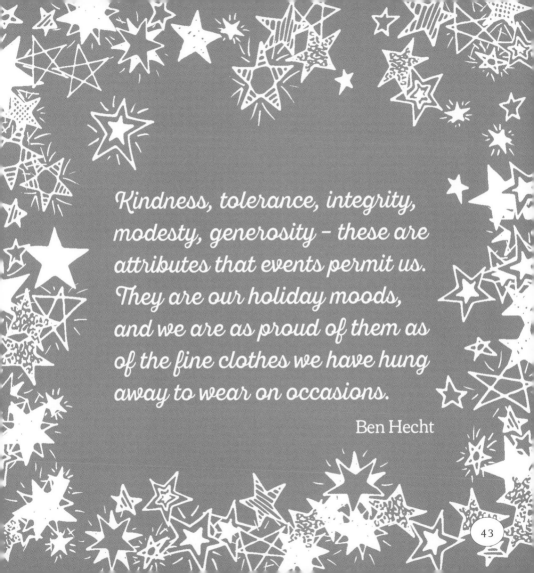

Kindness, tolerance, integrity, modesty, generosity – these are attributes that events permit us. They are our holiday moods, and we are as proud of them as of the fine clothes we have hung away to wear on occasions.

Ben Hecht

43

One of the toughest things for leaders to master is kindness. Kindness shares credit and offers enthusiastic praise for others' work. It's a balancing act between being genuinely kind and not looking weak.

Travis Bradberry

Tenderness is the name for a lover's most exquisite sensation; protection is implied in his most generous and heart-thrilling impulse.

William Godwin

That's what I consider true generosity: You give your all, and yet you always feel as if it costs you nothing.

Simone de Beauvoir

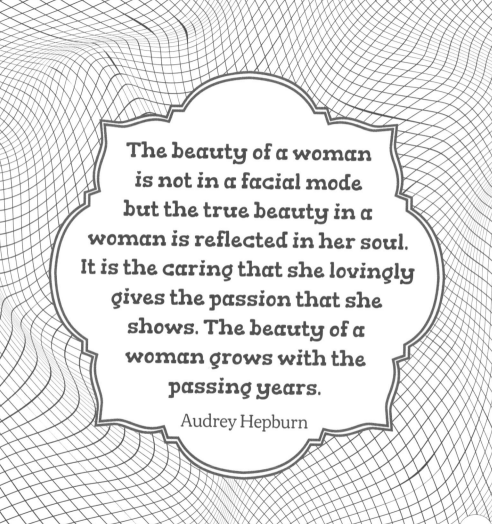

The beauty of a woman
is not in a facial mode
but the true beauty in a
woman is reflected in her soul.
It is the caring that she lovingly
gives the passion that she
shows. The beauty of a
woman grows with the
passing years.

Audrey Hepburn

*The deed is everything,
the glory naught.*

Johann Wolfgang
von Goethe

**The dew of
compassion
is a tear.**

Lord Byron

The greatness of a man is measured by the way he treats the little man. Compassion for the weak is a sign of greatness.

Myles Munroe

The heart benevolent
   and kind
The most resembles
   God.
Robert Burns

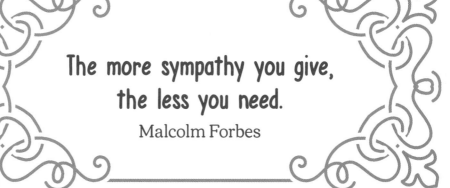

The more sympathy you give,
the less you need.

Malcolm Forbes

The true humanist maintains a just balance between sympathy and selection.

Irving Babbitt

There is an organic affinity
between joyousness and
tenderness, and their
companionship in the
saintly life need in no way
occasion surprise.

William James

There never was any heart
truly great and generous,
that was not also tender
and compassionate.

Robert Frost

'Tis the most tender part of love, each other to forgive.

John Sheffield

To desire and expect nothing for oneself and to have profound sympathy for others is genuine holiness.

Ivan Turgenev

To feel much for others and little for ourselves; to restrain our selfishness and exercise our benevolent affections, constitute the perfection of human nature.

Adam Smith

To remove ignorance
is an important branch
of benevolence.

Ann Plato

True compassion means not only feeling another's pain but also being moved to help relieve it.

Daniel Goleman

What does love look like? It has the hands to help others. It has the feet to hasten to the poor and needy. It has eyes to see misery and want. It has the ears to hear the sighs and sorrows of men. That is what love looks like.

Saint Augustine

When autumn darkness falls, what we will remember are the small acts of kindness: a cake, a hug, an invitation to talk, and every single rose. These are all expressions of a nation coming together and caring about its people.

Jens Stoltenberg

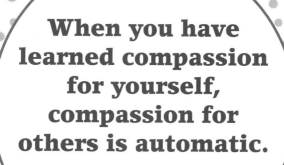

When you have learned compassion for yourself, compassion for others is automatic.

Henepola Gunaratana

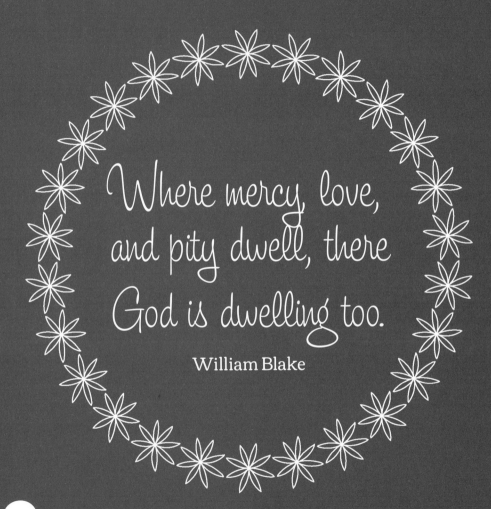

Where mercy, love,
and pity dwell, there
God is dwelling too.

William Blake

Wisdom, compassion and courage are the three universally recognised moral qualities of men.

Confucius

You may call God love, you may call
God goodness. But the best name for
God is compassion.

Meister Eckhart

THE VALUE OF KINDNESS

The simplest acts of kindness are by far more powerful than a thousand heads bowing in prayer.

Mahatma Gandhi

66

A tree is known by its fruit; a man by his deeds. A good deed is never lost; he who sows courtesy reaps friendship, and he who plants kindness gathers love.

Saint Basil

Compassion will cure more sins than condemnation.

Henry Ward Beecher

The best portion of a good man's life, his little, nameless, unremembered acts of kindness and of love.

William Wordsworth

I have always found that mercy bears richer fruits than strict justice.

Abraham Lincoln

I have found that among its other benefits, giving liberates the soul of the giver.

Maya Angelou

A laugh, to be joyous, must flow from a joyous heart, for without kindness, there can be no true joy.

Thomas Carlyle

A little thought and a little kindness are often worth more than a great deal of money.

John Ruskin

And as I've gotten older, I've had more of a tendency to look for people who live by kindness, tolerance, compassion, a gentler way of looking at things.

Martin Scorsese

At the end of the day, love and compassion will win.

Terry Waite

Compassion alone stands apart from the continuous traffic between good and evil proceeding within us.

Eric Hoffer

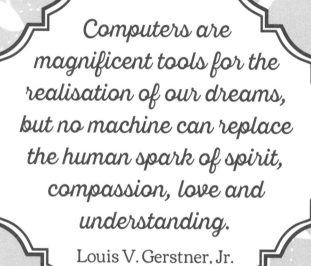

Computers are magnificent tools for the realisation of our dreams, but no machine can replace the human spark of spirit, compassion, love and understanding.

Louis V. Gerstner, Jr.

Constant kindness can accomplish much. As the sun makes ice melt, kindness causes misunderstanding, mistrust, and hostility to evaporate.

Albert Schweitzer

Feeling compassion for ourselves in no way releases us from responsibility for our actions. Rather, it releases us from the self-hatred that prevents us from responding to our life with clarity and balance.

Tara Brach

For it is in giving
that we receive.

Francis of Assisi

**General benevolence,
but not general
friendship, made a
man what he ought
to be.**

Jane Austen

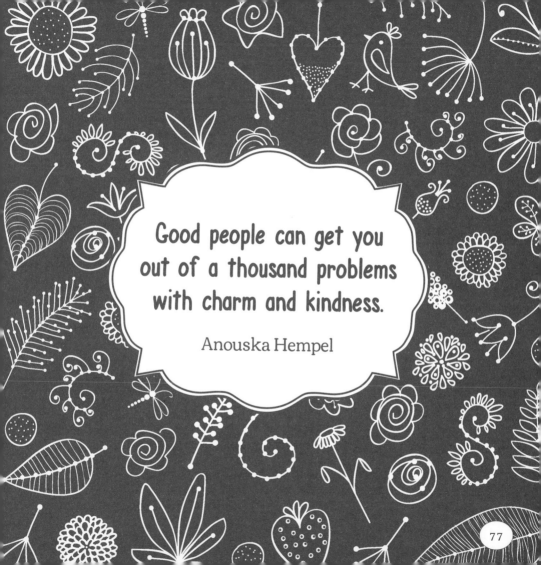

Good people can get you out of a thousand problems with charm and kindness.

Anouska Hempel

Here are the values that I stand for: honesty, equality, kindness, compassion, treating people the way you want to be treated and helping those in need. To me, those are traditional values.

Ellen DeGeneres

Honesty is the quality I value most in a friend. Not bluntness, but honesty with compassion.

Brooke Shields

I don't believe that directors need to essentially manipulate actors into doing things. You can suffer for your art, and you can make your own self suffer for your art. You don't need anyone else to do it for you. I work best when there's a safety trampoline of kindness.

Ruth Negga

I feel no need for any other faith than my faith in the kindness of human beings. I am so absorbed in the wonder of earth and the life upon it that I cannot think of heaven and angels.

Pearl S. Buck

I have understood that the most important things are tenderness and kindness. I can't do without them.

Brigitte Bardot

I learned far too
late in life that a long list
of letters after someone's
name is no guarantee of
compassion, kindness,
humour, all the far more
relevant stuff.

Bill Nighy

If a man sets his heart
on benevolence he will
be free from evil.

Confucius

If what must
be given is
given willingly
the kindness
is doubled.

Publilius Syrus

In giving freedom to the slave, we assure freedom to the free – honorable alike in that we give and what we preserve. We shall nobly save, or meanly lose, the last best hope of earth.

Abraham Lincoln

It's not how much we give but
how much love we put into giving.

Mother Teresa

Kind words do not cost much.
Yet they accomplish much.

Blaise Pascal

Kindness and faithfulness keep a king safe, through kindness his throne is made secure.

King Solomon

Kindness and politeness are not overrated at all. They're underused.

Tommy Lee Jones

86

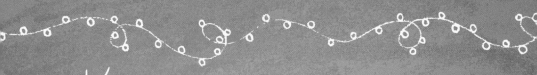

Kindness can become its own motive. We are made kind by being kind.

Eric Hoffer

Kindness eases everything almost as much as money does.

Mason Cooley

87

Kindness in
women, not their
beauteous looks, shall
win my love.

Washington Irving

Kindness in words creates
confidence. Kindness
in thinking creates
profoundness. Kindness in
giving creates love.

Lao Tzu

Kindness is always fashionable, and always welcome.

Amelia Barr

Kindness is more important than wisdom, and the recognition of this is the beginning of wisdom.

Theodore Isaac Rubin

Kindness is really important to me in finding my own prince – so are patience and a sense of humor. Without those qualities he's no Prince Charming!

Anne Hathaway

Kindness makes a fellow feel good whether it's being done to him or by him.

Frank A. Clark

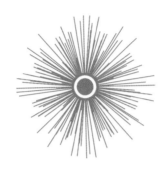

Life is made up, not of great sacrifices or duties, but of little things, in which smiles and kindness, and small obligations given habitually, are what preserve the heart and secure comfort.

Humphry Davy

Love and compassion are
necessities, not luxuries. Without
them humanity cannot survive.

Dalai Lama

Love and kindness are never wasted. They always make a difference. They bless the one who receives them, and they bless you, the giver.

Barbara De Angelis

Many men fail because they do not see the importance of being kind and courteous to the men under them. Kindness to everybody always pays for itself. And, besides, it is a pleasure to be kind.

Charles M. Schwab

Most of the good things that have happened to me, happened by accident when I was trying to help someone else.

Frank A. Clark

No act of kindness, no matter how small, is ever wasted.

Aesop

No one has ever become poor by giving.

Anne Frank

No one has yet realized the wealth of sympathy, the kindness and generosity hidden in the soul of a child. The effort of every true education should be to unlock that treasure.

Emma Goldman

**No one is useless
in this world
who lightens
the burdens of
another.**

Charles Dickens

None is so near the gods as he who
shows kindness.

Lucius Seneca

Nothing can make
injustice just but mercy.

Robert Frost

**One must be
poor to know the
luxury of giving.**

George Eliot

Our human compassion binds us the one to the other – not in pity or patronizingly, but as human beings who have learnt how to turn our common suffering into hope for the future.

Nelson Mandela

Our lack of forgiveness makes us hate, and our lack of compassion makes us hard-hearted. Pride in our hearts makes us resentful and keeps our memory in a constant whirlwind of passion and self-pity.

Mother Angelica

Paradise was made for tender hearts; hell, for loveless hearts.

Voltaire

Remember there's no such thing as a small act of kindness. Every act creates a ripple with no logical end.

Scott Adams

Remember this. Hold on to this. This is the only perfection there is, the perfection of helping others. This is the only thing we can do that has any lasting meaning. This is why we're here. To make each other feel safe.

Andre Agassi

Rich gifts wax poor when
givers prove unkind.

William Shakespeare

The drying up a single
tear has more of
honest fame than
shedding seas of gore.

Lord Byron

The end result of kindness is that it draws people to you.

Anita Roddick

The everyday kindness of the back roads more than makes up for the acts of greed in the headlines.

Charles Kuralt

The Gross National Product measures neither our wit nor our courage, neither our wisdom nor our learning, neither our compassion nor our devotion to our country. It measures everything, in short, except that which makes life worthwhile, and it can tell us everything about America - except whether we are proud to be Americans.

Robert Kennedy

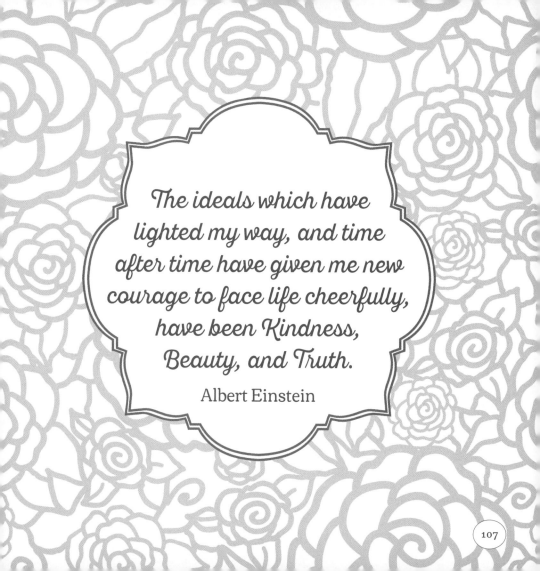

The ideals which have lighted my way, and time after time have given me new courage to face life cheerfully, have been Kindness, Beauty, and Truth.

Albert Einstein

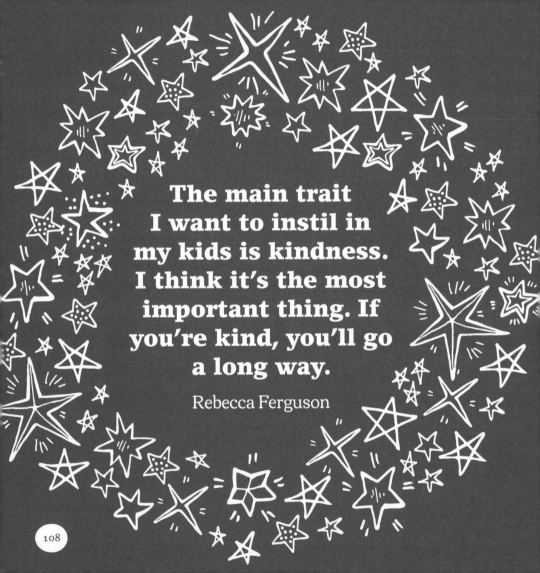

The main trait
I want to instil in
my kids is kindness.
I think it's the most
important thing. If
you're kind, you'll go
a long way.

Rebecca Ferguson

The man who practises unselfishness, who is genuinely interested in the welfare of others, who feels it a privilege to have the power to do a fellow-creature a kindness – even though polished manners and a gracious presence may be absent – will be an elevating influence wherever he goes.

Orison Swett Marden

The manner of giving is worth more than the gift.

Pierre Corneille

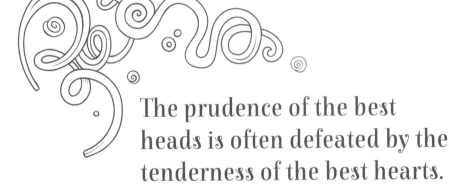

The prudence of the best heads is often defeated by the tenderness of the best hearts.

Henry Fielding

The purpose of life is not to be happy. It is to be useful, to be honorable, to be compassionate, to have it make some difference that you have lived and lived well.

Ralph Waldo Emerson

The qualities I most admire in women are confidence and kindness.

Oscar de la Renta

The words of kindness are more healing to a drooping heart than balm or honey.

Sarah Fielding

There are no greater treasures than the highest human qualities such as compassion, courage and hope. Not even tragic accident or disaster can destroy such treasures of the heart.

Daisaku Ikeda

**There is no charm equal
to tenderness of heart.**

Jane Austen

There is no exercise better
for the heart than reaching
down and lifting people up.

John Holmes

There's nothing so kingly
as kindness, and nothing
so royal as truth.

Alice Cary

Those who are
happiest are those
who do the most
for others

Booker T. Washington

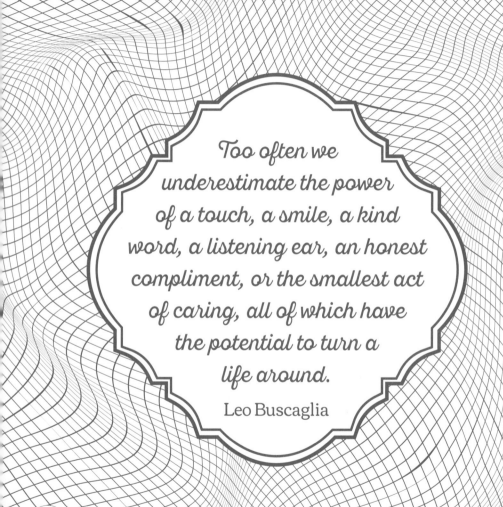

Too often we underestimate the power of a touch, a smile, a kind word, a listening ear, an honest compliment, or the smallest act of caring, all of which have the potential to turn a life around.

Leo Buscaglia

True beauty is born
through our actions
and aspirations and
in the kindness we
offer to others.

Alek Wek

True popularity comes from
acts of kindness rather than
acts of stupidity.

Bo Bennett

We are constituted so that simple acts of kindness, such as giving to charity or expressing gratitude, have a positive effect on our long-term moods. The key to the happy life, it seems, is the good life: a life with sustained relationships, challenging work, and connections to community.

Paul Bloom

We only have
what we give.

Isabel Allende

**What a liberating
thing to realize that our
problems are probably our
richest sources for rising
to the ultimate virtue of
compassion.**

Krista Tippett

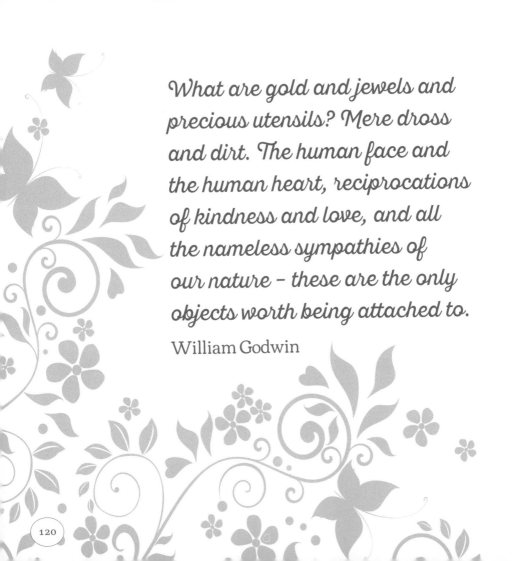

What are gold and jewels and precious utensils? Mere dross and dirt. The human face and the human heart, reciprocations of kindness and love, and all the nameless sympathies of our nature – these are the only objects worth being attached to.

William Godwin

What wisdom can you find that is greater than kindness?

Jean-Jacques Rousseau

Whatever possession we gain by our sword cannot be sure or lasting, but the love gained by kindness and moderation is certain and durable.

Alexander the Great

When death, the great reconciler, has come, it is never our tenderness that we repent of, but our severity.

George Eliot

When I was young, I admired clever people. Now that I am old, I admire kind people.

Abraham Joshua Heschel

When you carry out acts of kindness you get a wonderful feeling inside. It is as though something inside your body responds and says, yes, this is how I ought to feel.

Harold Kushner

When you treat yourself with the kindness and high regard that you would give to one of your spiritual heroes, your body becomes the epicenter of quiet joy rather than a battlefield for the ego.

Debbie Ford

Where there is no human connection, there is no compassion. Without compassion, then community, commitment, loving-kindness, human understanding, and peace all shrivel. Individuals become isolated, the isolated turn cruel, and the tragic hovers in the forms of domestic and civil violence. Art and literature are antidotes to that.

Susan Vreeland

Wise sayings often fall on barren ground;
but a kind word is never thrown away.

Sir Arthur Helps

Without tenderness, a
man is uninteresting.

Marlene Dietrich

You can accomplish by kindness
what you cannot by force.

Publilius Syrus

**You can be rich in spirit,
kindness, love and all
those things that you
can't put a dollar sign on.**

Dolly Parton

You either believe that people respond to authority, or that they respond to kindness and inclusion. I'm obviously in the latter camp. I think that people respond better to reward than punishment.

Brian Eno

KINDNESS AS SOCIAL RESPONSIBILITY

It is in our faults
and failings, not in our
virtues, that we touch each
other, and find sympathy.
It is in our follies that
we are one.

Jerome K. Jerome

Kindness is in our power, even when fondness is not.

Samuel Johnson

Life's persistent and most urgent question is 'What are you doing for others?'

Martin Luther King, Jr.

Man's inhumanity to man makes countless thousands mourn!

Robert Burns

A little anger is a good thing if it isn't on your own behalf, if it's for others deserving of your anger, your empathy.

David Simon

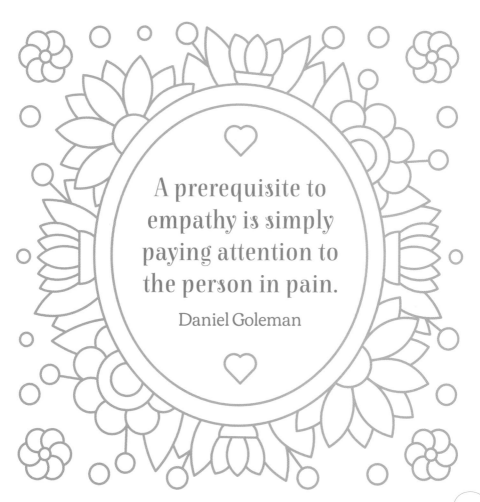

A prerequisite to empathy is simply paying attention to the person in pain.

Daniel Goleman

A spirit, breathing the language of independence, is natural to Englishmen, few of whom are disposed to brook compulsion, or submit to the dictates of others, when not softened by reason, or tempered with kindness.

Joseph Lancaster

As we grow in our consciousness, there will be more compassion and more love, and then the barriers between people, between religions, between nations will begin to fall.

Ram Dass

Be kind to unkind people ~ they need it the most.

Ashleigh Brilliant

Cowards are cruel, but the brave love mercy and delight to save.

John Gay

Day after day, ordinary people become heroes through extraordinary and selfless actions to help their neighbours.

Sylvia Mathews Burwell

Desperation, weakness, vulnerability – these things will always be exploited. You need to protect the weak, ring-fence them, with something far stronger than empathy.

Zadie Smith

**Difficult as it is really
to listen to someone in affliction,
it is just as difficult for him
to know that compassion is
listening to him.**

Simone Weil

Do not ask the name
of the person who asks you for
a bed for the night. He whose
name is a burden to him needs
shelter more than anyone.

Victor Hugo

Each time a man stands up for an ideal, or acts to improve the lot of others, or strikes out against injustice, he sends forth a tiny ripple of hope, and crossing each other from a million different centers of energy and daring, those ripples build a current that can sweep down the mightiest walls of oppression and resistance.

Robert Kennedy

Every man must decide
whether he will walk in the
light of creative altruism
or in the darkness of
destructive selfishness.

Martin Luther King, Jr.

Give what you have. To someone, it may be better than you dare to think.

Henry Wadsworth Longfellow

God's dream is
that you and I and all
of us will realise that we
are family, that we are made
for togetherness, for goodness
and for compassion.

Desmond Tutu

Having levelled my palace, don't erect a hovel and complacently admire your own charity in giving me that for a home.

Emily Brontë

He has a right to criticize, who has a heart to help.

Abraham Lincoln

How far you go in life depends on your being tender with the young, compassionate with the aged, sympathetic with the striving and tolerant of the weak and strong. Because someday in your life you will have been all of these.

George Washington Carver

Human kindness has never weakened the stamina or softened the fibre of a free people. A nation does not have to be cruel to be tough.

Franklin D. Roosevelt

Human nature is complex. Even if we do have inclinations toward violence, we also have inclination to empathy, to cooperation, to self-control.

Steven Pinker

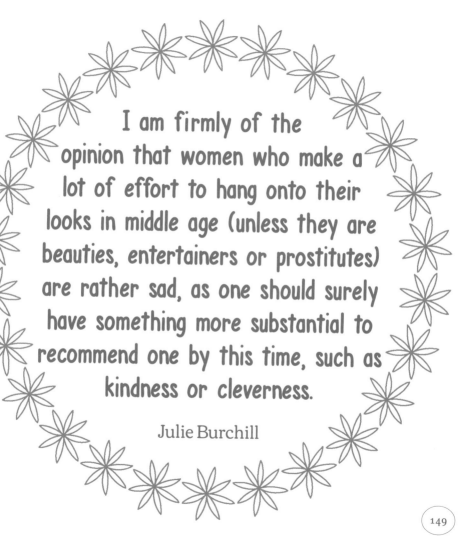

I am firmly of the opinion that women who make a lot of effort to hang onto their looks in middle age (unless they are beauties, entertainers or prostitutes) are rather sad, as one should surely have something more substantial to recommend one by this time, such as kindness or cleverness.

Julie Burchill

I have always
depended on the kindness
of strangers.

Tennessee Williams

I have no idea
what's awaiting me, or
what will happen when this all
ends. For the moment I know this:
there are sick people and they
need curing.

Albert Camus

I like kindness. Who doesn't?
Life is definitely too short for
self-centered, abusive people.

Ellen Greene

*I think one of the best words
in the English language is 'compassion.'
I think it holds everything. It holds love,
it holds care... and if everybody just did
something. We all make a difference.*

Michael Crawford

I think we all have empathy. We may not have enough courage to display it.

Maya Angelou

I'm doing everything that I can, working with experts, really studying the statistics to figure out a way we can make it cool or normal to be kind and loving.

Lady Gaga

If our wondrous kindness is evidence for God, is our capacity for great evil proof of the Devil?

Paul Bloom

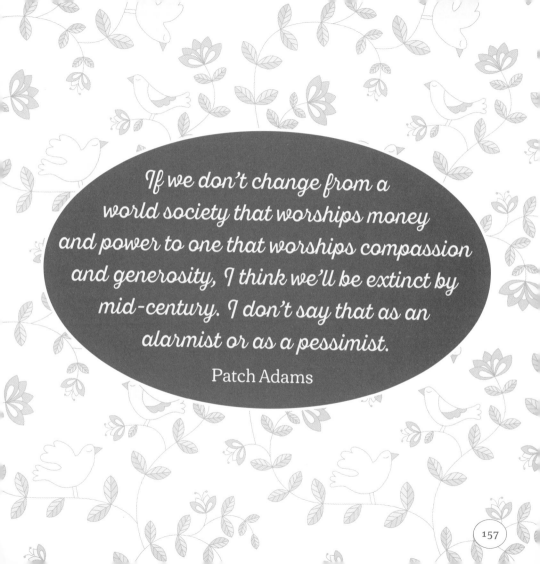

If we don't change from a world society that worships money and power to one that worships compassion and generosity, I think we'll be extinct by mid-century. I don't say that as an alarmist or as a pessimist.

Patch Adams

If you list the qualities that we consider feminine, they are patience, understanding, empathy, supportiveness, a desire to nurture. Our culture tells us those are feminine traits, but they're really just human.

Sydney Pollack

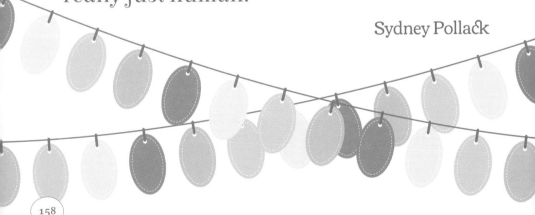

In the face of unspeakable evil, our whole nation must respond with countless acts of kindness, warmth and generosity.

Steve Scalise

It takes generosity to discover the whole through others. If you realize you are only a violin, you can open yourself up to the world by playing your role in the concert.

Jacques Yves Cousteau

It's not our job to play judge and jury, to determine who is worthy of our kindness and who is not. We just need to be kind, unconditionally and without ulterior motive, even – or rather, especially – when we'd prefer not to be.

Josh Radnor

Kindly words do not enter so deeply into men as a reputation for kindness.

Mencius

Kindness has converted more sinners than zeal, eloquence or learning.

Frederick William Faber

Never respect men merely for their riches, but rather for their philanthropy; we do not value the sun for its height, but for its use.

Gamaliel Bailey

No deep and strong feeling, such as we may come across here and there in the world, is unmixed with compassion. The more we love, the more the object of our love seems to us to be a victim.

Boris Pasternak

Not for ourselves alone are we born.

Marcus Tullius Cicero

Nothing graces the Christian soul so much as mercy; mercy as shown chiefly towards the poor, that thou mayest treat them as sharers in common with thee in the produce of nature, which brings forth the fruits of the earth for use to all.

Saint Ambrose

Obviously, you would give
your life for your children, or give
them the last biscuit on the plate. But
to me, the trick in life is to take that sense
of generosity between kin, make it apply
to the extended family and to your
neighbour, your village
and beyond.

Tom Stoppard

Oh! if the good hearts had the fat purses, how much better everything would go!

Victor Hugo

One who knows how to show and to accept kindness will be a friend better than any possession.

Sophocles

Our prime purpose in this life is to help others. And if you can't help them, at least don't hurt them.

Dalai Lama

Remember that the happiest people are not those getting more, but those giving more.

H. Jackson Brown, Jr.

Somewhere near you,
somebody right now
is trying to help the
indigent and poor –
providing food, shelter,
clothing or simple
kindness.

Tony Snow

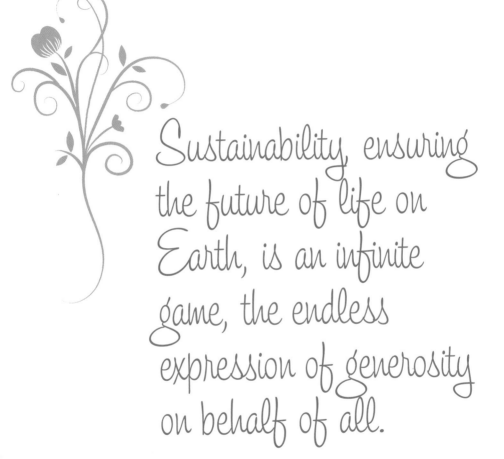

Sustainability, ensuring the future of life on Earth, is an infinite game, the endless expression of generosity on behalf of all.

Paul Hawken

Teetotallers lack the
sympathy and generosity
of men that drink.

W. H. Davies

The bravest are the
most tender; the loving
are the daring.

Bayard Taylor

The delicate balance of mentoring someone is not creating them in your own image, but giving them the opportunity to create themselves.

Steven Spielberg

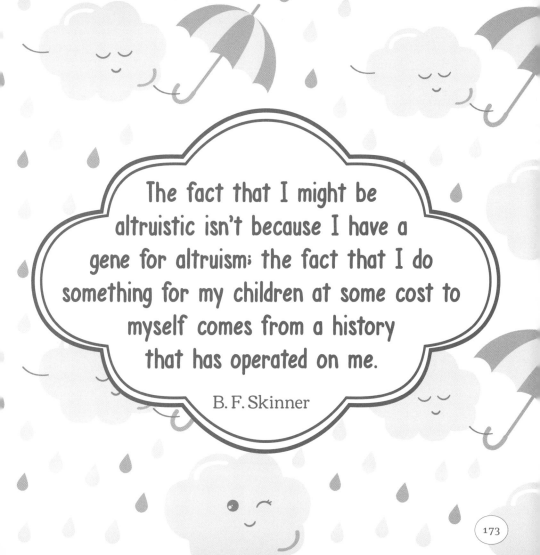

The fact that I might be altruistic isn't because I have a gene for altruism; the fact that I do something for my children at some cost to myself comes from a history that has operated on me.

B. F. Skinner

173

The good in this world far outweighs the evil. Our common humanity transcends our differences, and our most effective response to terror is compassion, it's unity, and it's love.

Loretta Lynch

The proper aim of giving is to put the recipient in a state where he no longer needs our gifts

C. S. Lewis

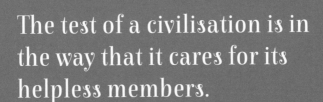

The test of a civilisation is in the way that it cares for its helpless members.

Pearl S. Buck

The Trail of Tears should teach all of us the importance of respect for others who are different from ourselves and compassion for those who have difficulties.

Joseph Bruchac

The way I stand up to bullies is with kindness and love. Because I think that's what they really need. They're misunderstood and probably really upset themselves.

Chrissy Metz

The youngest children have a great
capacity for empathy and altruism.
There's a recent study that shows even
14-month-olds will climb across a bunch
of cushions and go across a room to
give you a pen if you drop one.

Alison Gopnik

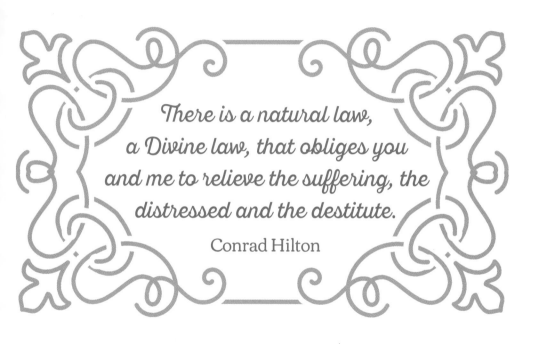

There is a natural law,
a Divine law, that obliges you
and me to relieve the suffering, the
distressed and the destitute.

Conrad Hilton

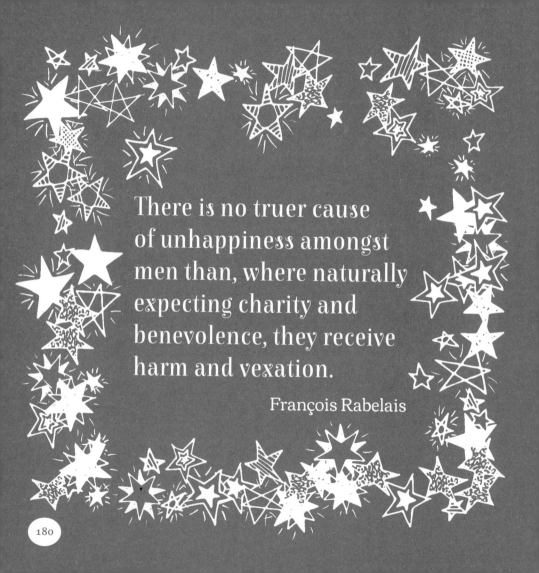

There is no truer cause
of unhappiness amongst
men than, where naturally
expecting charity and
benevolence, they receive
harm and vexation.

François Rabelais

There's no dearth of kindness In the world of ours; Only in our blindness We gather thorns for flowers.

T. G. Massey

'Tis not enough to help the feeble up but to support him after.

William Shakespeare

181

To pity distress
is but human;
to relieve it is
Godlike.

Horace Mann

Today we are afraid of simple words
like goodness and mercy and kindness.
We don't believe in the good old words
because we don't believe in good old values
anymore. And that's why the world is sick.

Lin Yutang

We can prevent many people from becoming terrorists by truly listening to people who feel they've been treated unjustly and responding to their concerns with a sense of justice and compassion.

Coretta Scott King

We cannot be kind to each other here for even an hour. We whisper, and hint, and chuckle and grin at our brother's shame; however you take it we men are a little breed.

Alfred Lord Tennyson

We who lived in concentration camps can remember the men who walked through the huts comforting others, giving away their last piece of bread.

Viktor E. Frankl

We're all generous, but with different things, like time, money, talent – criticism.

Frank A. Clark

Wealth is not to feed our egos but to feed the hungry and to help people help themselves.

Andrew Carnegie

What I hope to promote is the idea that we all need each other and that the greatest happiness in life is not how much we have but how much we give. That's a wealth that's priceless.

Herbie Hancock

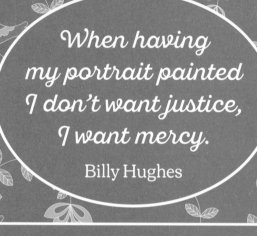

*When having
my portrait painted
I don't want justice,
I want mercy.*

Billy Hughes

When we're looking for compassion, we need someone who is deeply rooted, is able to bend and, most of all, embraces us for our strengths and struggles.

Brene Brown

When will our consciences grow so tender that we will act to prevent human misery rather than avenge it?

Eleanor Roosevelt

When you are kind to someone in trouble, you hope they'll remember and be kind to someone else. And it'll become like a wildfire.

Whoopi Goldberg

Whether one believes in a religion or not, and whether one believes in rebirth or not, there isn't anyone who doesn't appreciate kindness and compassion.

Dalai Lama

You often say; I would give, but only to the deserving,

The trees in your orchard say not so, nor the flocks in your pasture.

Surely he who is worthy to receive his days and nights is worthy of all else from you.

Kahlil Gibran

You have not lived today
until you have done
something for someone who
can never repay you.

John Bunyan

We are all here on earth to help
others; what on earth the others
are here for I don't know.

W. H. Auden

TOUGH LOVE

"I don't feel very much like Pooh today," said Pooh.
"There there," said Piglet.
"I'll bring you tea and honey until you do."

A. A. Milne

A person who has good thoughts cannot ever be ugly. You can have a wonky nose and a crooked mouth and a double chin and stick-out teeth, but if you have good thoughts they will shine out of your face like sunbeams and you will always look lovely.

Roald Dahl

A benevolent mind, and the face
assumes the patterns of benevolence.
An evil mind, then an evil face.

Jimmy Sangster

A good commander is
benevolent and unconcerned
with fame.

Sun Tzu

'A man must have something to grumble about; and if he can't complain that his wife harries him to death with her perversity and ill-humour, he must complain that she wears him out with her kindness and gentleness.

Anne Brontë

A word of kindness is seldom
spoken in vain, while witty
sayings are as easily lost as
the pearls slipping from a
broken string.

George Dennison Prentice

198

And in our world
    of plenty we must
    spread a smile of joy
Throw your arms
    around the world at
    Christmas time.

Bob Geldof and Midge Ure

Come, gentlemen, I hope we
shall drink down all unkindness.

William Shakespeare

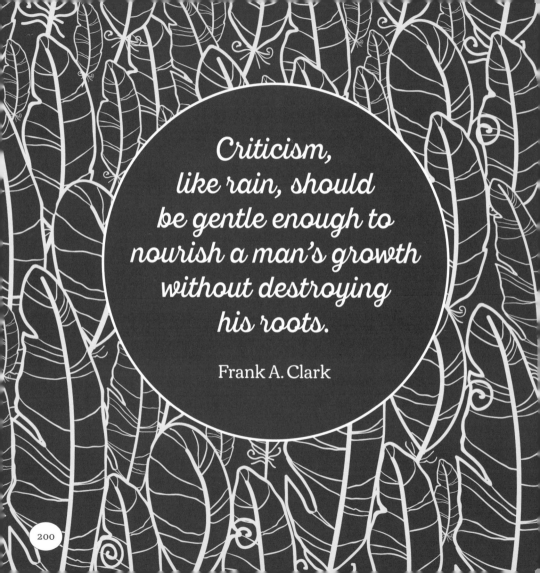

Criticism,
like rain, should
be gentle enough to
nourish a man's growth
without destroying
his roots.

Frank A. Clark

Do you know what it means to come home at night to a woman who'll give you a little love, a little affection, a little tenderness?

It means you're in the wrong house, that's what it means.

Henny Youngman

Entrepreneurs may be brutally honest,
but fostering relationships with partners
and building enduring communities
requires empathy, self-sacrifice and
a willingness to help others without
expecting anything in return.

Ben Parr

Every day, some act of kindness comes my way, even if it's just someone opening the door. It happens every day if you keep an eye out for it. Keeping an eye out, that's the key.

Aaron Neville

For auld lang syne, my dear, for auld lang syne, We'll take a cup of kindness yet for auld lang syne.

Robert Burns

For Brutus, as you know,
  was Caesar's angel.
Judge, *O you gods*, how
  dearly Caesar lov'd him!
This was the most
  unkindest cut of all;
For when the noble Caesar
  saw him stab,
Ingratitude, more strong
  than traitors' arms,
Quite vanquish'd him: then
  burst his mighty heart.

William Shakespeare

Generosity is nothing else than a craze to possess. All which I abandon, all which I give, I enjoy in a higher manner through the fact that I give it away. To give is to enjoy possessively the object which one gives.

Jean-Paul Sartre

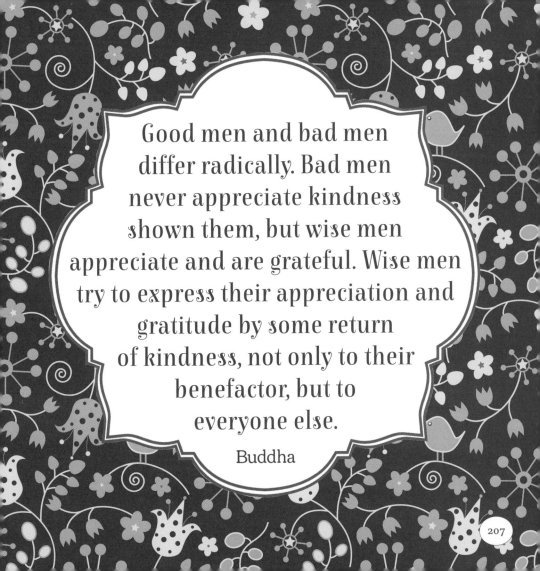

Good men and bad men differ radically. Bad men never appreciate kindness shown them, but wise men appreciate and are grateful. Wise men try to express their appreciation and gratitude by some return of kindness, not only to their benefactor, but to everyone else.

Buddha

Difficulty creates the opportunity for self-reflection and compassion.

Suzan-Lori Parks

Greed has poisoned men's souls, has barricaded the world with hate, has goose-stepped us into misery and bloodshed.

We have developed speed, but we have shut ourselves in. Machinery that gives abundance has left us in want. Our knowledge has made us cynical; our cleverness, hard and unkind. We think too much and feel too little. More than machinery, we need humanity. More than cleverness, we need kindness and gentleness. Without these qualities, life will be violent and all will be lost.

Charlie Chaplin

Grief can be the garden of compassion. If you keep your heart open through everything, your pain can become your greatest ally in your life's search for love and wisdom.

Rumi

Here bring your wounded
   hearts, here tell your anguish;
Earth has no sorrow that
   Heaven cannot heal.

Thomas Moore

*Here is my secret. It is very simple: It is
only with the heart that one can see rightly;
what is essential is invisible to the eye.*

Antoine de Saint-Exupéry

How beautiful a
day can be
When kindness
touches it!

George Elliston

Human judges can show mercy. But against
the laws of nature, there is no appeal.

Arthur C. Clarke

By ventilation units where towers
   meet the street
The ragged stand in bags soaking
   heat up through their feet
This was the only kindness, it
   was accidental too...

The Clash

Human kindness is like a
defective tap; the first gush
may be impressive but the
stream soon dries up.

P. D. James

213

I am unjust,
but I can strive for justice.
My life's unkind, but I can
vote for kindness.
I, the unloving, say life
should be lovely.
I, that am blind, cry out
against my blindness.

Vachel Lindsay

I believe we are still so innocent. The species are still so innocent that a person who is apt to be murdered believes that the murderer, just before he puts the final wrench on his throat, will have enough compassion to give him one sweet cup of water.

Maya Angelou

I expect to pass through life but once. If therefore, there be any kindness I can show, or any good thing I can do to any fellow being, let me do it now, and not defer or neglect it, as I shall not pass this way again.

William Penn

I have learned silence from the talkative, toleration from the intolerant, and kindness from the unkind; yet, strange, I am ungrateful to those teachers.

Kahlil Gibran

I will not call that person happy who
knows no rest because of his enemies,
who is the butt of fun by all and for
whom no one has any empathy, who is
as if held on a leash by others, who has
lost himself in hedonistic pursuits, who
preys on those weaker to him and wags
his tail for his superiors.

Munshi Premchand

I've never known any human being, high or humble, who ever regretted, when nearing life's end, having done kindly deeds. But I have known more than one millionaire who became haunted by the realization that they had led selfish lives.

B. C. Forbes

"Pooh, promise me you won't forget about me, ever. Not even when I'm a hundred."

Pooh thought for a little.

"How old shall I be then?"

"Ninety-nine."

Pooh nodded.

"I promise," he said.

A. A. Milne

If nature has made you for a giver, your hands are born open, and so is your heart; and though there may be times when your hands are empty, your heart is always full, and you can give things out of that - warm things, kind things, sweet things - help and comfort and laughter - and sometimes gay, kind laughter is the best help of all.

Frances Hodgson Burnett

If you haven't any charity in your heart, you have the worst kind of heart trouble.

Bob Hope

If you stop to be kind, you must swerve often from your path.

Mary Webb

Ignorant kindness may have the effect of cruelty; but to be angry with it as if it were direct cruelty would be an ignorant unkindness.

George Eliot

In human relationships, kindness and lies are worth a thousand truths.

Graham Greene

It is only after one is in trouble that one realises how little sympathy and kindness there are in the world.

Nellie Bly

It is sometimes difficult to view compassion and loving kindness as the strengths they are.

Sharon Salzberg

It was good to learn so early. They're not going to be kind to you. You have to do it and get on, and then gulp down and get better.

Judi Dench

Just for today, I will let go of anger.
Just for today, I will let go of worry.
Today, I will count my many blessings.
Today, I will do my work honestly.
Today, I will be kind to every living creature.

Mikao Usui

Kind words are short and easy to speak, but their echoes are truly endless.

Mother Teresa

Dame Kindness, she is
so nice!

The blue and red jewels
of her rings smoke

In the windows, the
mirrors

Are filling with smiles.

Sylvia Plath

227

Kindness is weak when you use it in a self-serving manner. Self-serving kindness is thin – people can see right through it when a kind leader has an agenda.

Travis Bradberry

Like a bridge over troubled water, I will lay me down.

Paul Simon

Love can be unselfish,
in the sense of being
benevolent and generous,
without being selfless.

Mortimer Adler

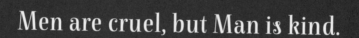

Men are cruel, but Man is kind.

Rabindranath Tagore

Men are more prone to revenge injuries than to requite kindness.

Thomas Fuller

Men who look on nature, and their fellow-men, and cry that all is dark and gloomy, are in the right; but the sombre colours are reflections from their own jaundiced eyes and hearts. The real hues are delicate, and need a clearer vision.

Charles Dickens

Not always actions show
the man; we find who does a
kindness is not therefore kind.

Alexander Pope

Nothing is black
or white, nothing's 'us
or them.' But then there are
magical, beautiful things in
the world. There's incredible
acts of kindness and bravery,
and in the most unlikely
places, and it gives
you hope.

Dave Matthews

Oh, she may be weary
Young girls they do get weary
Wearing that same old shaggy dress
But when she gets weary
Try a little tenderness.

Otis Redding

Oh, why you look so sad, the tears
are in your eyes
Come on and come to me now,
and don't be ashamed to cry
Let me see you through, 'cause
I've seen the dark side too
When the night falls on you, you
don't know what to do
Nothing you confess could make
me love you less, I'll stand by you.

The Pretenders

One could laugh at the world better if it didn't mix tender kindliness with its brutality.

D. H. Lawrence

Only a kind person is able to judge another justly and to make allowances for his weaknesses. A kind eye, while recognising defects, sees beyond them.

Lawrence G. Lovasik

Our brand of democracy is hard. But I can promise that a year from now, when I no longer hold this office, I'll be right there with you as a citizen – inspired by those voices of fairness and vision, of grit and good humour and kindness that have helped America travel so far.

Barack Obama

Resilience is, of course, necessary for a warrior. But a lack of empathy isn't.

Phil Klay

Self-pity comes so naturally to all of us. The most solid happiness can be shaken by the compassion of a fool.

André Maurois

Shall we make a new
rule of life from tonight:
always to try to be a little
kinder than is necessary?

J. M. Barrie

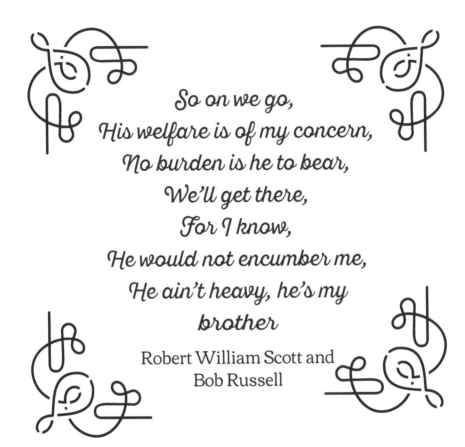

So on we go,
His welfare is of my concern,
No burden is he to bear,
We'll get there,
For I know,
He would not encumber me,
He ain't heavy, he's my
brother

Robert William Scott and
Bob Russell

Sometimes people don't trust the force of kindness. They think love or compassion or kindness will make you weak and kind of stupid and people will take advantage of you; you won't stand up for other people.

Sharon Salzberg

The nicest feeling in the world is to do a good deed anonymously - and have somebody find out.

Oscar Wilde

The pleasure we derive from doing favors is partly in the feeling it gives us that we are not altogether worthless. It is a pleasant surprise to ourselves.

Eric Hoffer

The problem with compassion
is that it is not photogenic.

Sebastian Horsley

The quality of mercy is
 not strain'd,
It droppeth as the gentle
 rain from heaven
Upon the place beneath:
 it is twice blest;
It blesseth him that
 gives and him that takes...

William Shakespeare

There is a rollicking kindness that looks like malice.

Friedrich Nietzsche

There is no sickness worse for me than words that to be kind must lie.

Aeschylus

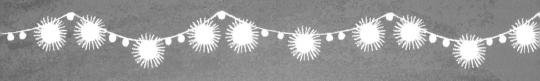

This is my simple religion. There is no need for temples; no need for complicated philosophy. Our own brain, our own heart is our temple the philosophy is kindness.

Dalai Lama

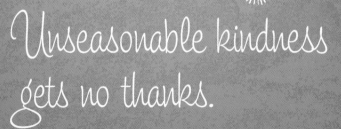

Unseasonable kindness gets no thanks.

Thomas Fuller

Vanity is as ill at ease under
indifference as tenderness is under
a love which it cannot return.

George Eliot

Verily the kindness that gazes
upon itself in a mirror turns to
stone, and a good deed that calls
itself by tender names becomes
the parent to a curse.

Kahlil Gibran

We win by tenderness.
We conquer by
forgiveness.

Frederick William Robertson

**We've put more effort
into helping folks
reach old age than
into helping them
enjoy it.**

Frank A. Clark

When kindness has left people, even for a few moments, we become afraid of them as if their reason had left them. When it has left a place where we have always found it, it is like shipwreck; we drop from security into something malevolent and bottomless.

Willa Cather

When someone is crying, of course, the noble thing to do is to comfort them. But if someone is trying to hide their tears, it may also be noble to pretend you do not notice them.

Lemony Snicket

When the night has come
And the land is dark
And the moon is the only light we'll see
No, I won't be afraid
Oh, I won't be afraid
Just as long as you stand
Stand by me

Ben E. King, Jerry Leiber
and Mike Stoller

When you're successful, people have no sympathy. Nobody wants to catch the tears of a millionaire.

Boy George

Where you tend a rose, my lad, a thistle cannot grow.

Frances Hodgson Burnett

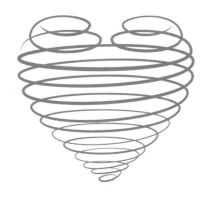

Yet do I fear thy nature;
It is too full o' th' milk of
human kindness.

William Shakespeare

"You have plenty of courage, I am sure," answered Oz. "All you need is confidence in yourself. There is no living thing that is not afraid when it faces danger. The true courage is in facing danger when you are afraid, and that kind of courage you have in plenty."

L. Frank Baum

Sympathy is the first
condition of criticism.

Henri Frederic Amiel

The greatest firmness
is the greatest mercy.

Henry Wadsworth Longfellow

I must be cruel, only to be kind.

William Shakespeare

THE KEY TO KINDNESS

A man there was, though some did count him mad. The more he cast away, the more he had.

John Bunyan

Be amusing: never tell unkind stories; above all, never tell long ones.

Benjamin Disraeli

Be generous with kindly words, especially about those who are absent.

Johann Wolfgang von Goethe

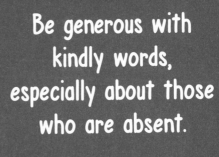

Be kind to people on the way up - you'll meet them again on your way down.

Jimmy Durante

Be kind whenever possible. It is always possible.

Dalai Lama

Be kind, for everyone you meet is fighting a hard battle.

Philo

"A fight is going on inside you,"
an old man said to his grandson.
"It is a fight between two wolves.
One wolf is evil. He is anger,
greed, envy, destruction and
lies. The other wolf is good. He is
joy, generosity, kindness, hope
and truth. These two wolves are
fighting inside you."
The grandson listened and
thought for a while, then asked,
"But which wolf will win?"
The old man replied,
"The one you feed."

Traditional

'A gentleman has his eyes on all those present; he is tender toward the bashful, gentle toward the distant, and merciful toward the absent.

Lawrence G. Lovasik

A good character is the best tombstone. Those who loved you and were helped by you will remember you when forget-me-nots have withered. Carve your name on hearts, not on marble.

Charles H. Spurgeon

A kindness received should be returned with a freer hand.

Saint Ambrose

A mistake made by many people with great convictions is that they will let nothing stand in the way of their views, not even kindness.

Bryant H. McGill

Always do good to others.
Be selfless. Mentally remove
everything and be free. This is
divine life. This is the direct
way to Moksha or salvation.

Swami Sivananda

An enemy to whom you show
kindness becomes your friend,
excepting lust, the indulgence
of which increases its enmity.

Saadi

As freely as the firmament embraces the world, or the sun pours forth impartially his beams, so mercy must encircle both friend and foe.

Friedrich Schiller

As much as we need a prosperous economy, we also need a prosperity of kindness and decency.

Caroline Kennedy

Because a human being is endowed with empathy, he violates the natural order if he does not reach out to those who need care.

Dayananda Saraswati

Beginning today, treat everyone you meet as if they were going to be dead by midnight. Extend to them all the care, kindness and understanding you can muster, and do it with no thought of any reward. Your life will never be the same again.

Og Mandino

Behold! I do not give
lectures or a little charity.
When I give I give myself.

Walt Whitman

Being generous often consists of simply extending a hand. That's hard to do if you are grasping tightly to your righteousness, your belief system, your superiority, your assumptions about others, your definition of normal.

Patti Digh

Both man and womankind
belie their nature when
they are not kind.

Philip James Bailey

Carry out a random act of kindness,
with no expectation of reward, safe in
the knowledge that one day someone
might do the same for you.

Princess Diana

Deliberately seek opportunities for kindness, sympathy, and patience.

Evelyn Underhill

Do not just seek happiness for yourself. Seek happiness for all. Through kindness. Through mercy.

David Levithan

Doing nothing for others is the undoing of ourselves.

Horace Mann

Every minute of every hour of every day you are making the world, just as you are making yourself, and you might as well do it with generosity and kindness and style.

Rebecca Solnit

First and foremost, we need to be the adults we want our children to be. We should watch our own gossiping and anger. We should model the kindness we want to see.

Brene Brown

Getting money is not all a man's business: to cultivate kindness is a valuable part of the business of life.

Samuel Johnson

Guard well within yourself that treasure, kindness. Know how to give without hesitation, how to lose without regret, how to acquire without meanness.

George Sand

Have you had a kindness shown?
Pass it on, pass it on!
'Twas not giv'n for thee alone,
Pass it on, pass it on!
Let it travel down the years,
Let it wipe another's tears;
'Till in heav'n the deed appears
Pass it on, pass it on!

Henry Burton

He that has done you a kindness will be more ready to do you another, than he whom you yourself have obliged.

Benjamin Franklin

He who aspires to paradise should learn to deal with people with kindness.

Abu Bakr

He who confers a favour
should at once forget
it, if he is not to show
a sordid ungenerous
spirit. To remind a man
of a kindness conferred
and to talk of it, is little
different from reproach.

Demosthenes

He who fears to weep, should learn to be kind to those who weep.

Abu Bakr

I cry a lot when I feel empathy. I can feel heartbroken by life, and I cry quite easily, sometimes for no reason. It's healthy, I think.

Bat for Lashes

I know you got
moutains to climb but
Always stay humble
and kind

Lori McKenna

I say to people who care for people who are dying, if you really love that person and want to help them, be with them when their end comes close. Sit with them – you don't even have to talk. You don't have to do anything but really be there with them.

Elisabeth Kubler-Ross

I think it's imperative to have faith or religion, because it's good to have morals, to be kind to others.

Tinie Tempah

I want everyone to know what they
deserve in relationships: that they can
demand equality and kindness. Because
everyone will have a relationship at
some point in their life. It's what we
all do, every day, and we need to know
how to do it.

Olivia Colman

I'm honest and fair, but I don't dispense false kindness.

Steve Easterbrook

I've been searching for ways to heal myself, and I've found that kindness is the best way.

Lady Gaga

If you expect the blessings of God, be kind to His people.

Abu Bakr

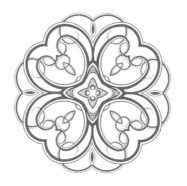

If you have an impulse to kindness, act on it.

Douglas Coupland

If you want to call attention to your good deed then it isn't a good deed, it's a self-serving one. Why? Not only have you patted yourself on the back but you're fishing for others to do the same.

Donna Lynn Hope

If you're not making someone else's life better, then you're wasting your time. Your life will become better by making other lives better.

Will Smith

Illness is the doctor to whom we pay most heed; to kindness, to knowledge we make promise only; pain we obey.

Marcel Proust

In giving advice seek to help, not to please, your friend.

Solon

It doesn't hurt to show some empathy.

John Cornyn

It takes a little bit of mindfulness and a little bit of attention to others to be a good listener, which helps cultivate emotional nurturing and engagement.

Deepak Chopra

289

It's bad enough in life to do without something YOU want; but confound it, what gets my goat is not being able to give somebody something you want THEM to have.

Truman Capote

Justice consists in doing no injury to men; decency in giving them no offense.

Marcus Tullius Cicero

Kind hearts are the gardens,
Kind thoughts are the roots,
Kind words are the flowers,
Kind deeds are the fruits,
Take care of your garden
And keep out the weeds,
Fill it with sunshine,
Kind words and kind deeds.

Henry Wadsworth Longfellow

Kings in this world should imitate God, their mercy should be above their works.

William Penn

Learn to know every man under you, get under his skin, know his faults. Then cater to him – with kindness or roughness as his case may demand.

John McGraw

Let us fill our hearts with our own compassion – towards ourselves and towards all living beings.

Thich Nhat Hanh

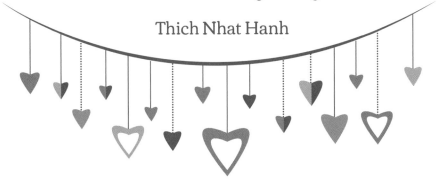

Love one another and help others to rise to the higher levels, simply by pouring out love. Love is infectious and the greatest healing energy.

Sai Baba

Make no judgements
where you have no
compassion.

Anne McCaffrey

Most comedy is based on getting a laugh at somebody else's expense. And I find that that's just a form of bullying in a major way. So I want to be an example that you can be funny and be kind, and make people laugh without hurting somebody else's feelings.

Ellen DeGeneres

My philosophy is that the most important aspect of any religion should be human kindness. And to try to ease the suffering of others. To try to bring light and love into the lives of mankind.

Steven Seagal

My religious philosophy is kindness. Try to be kind. That's something worth achieving.

Pierce Brosnan

Oh be swift to love,
make haste to be kind.

Henri Frederic Amiel

One who is kind is sympathetic and gentle with others. He is considerate of others' feelings and courteous in his behavior. He has a helpful nature. Kindness pardons others' weaknesses and faults. Kindness is extended to all – to the aged and the young, to animals, to those low of station as well as the high.

Ezra Taft Benson

One's life has value so long as
one attributes value to the life of
others, by means of love, friendship,
indignation and compassion.

Simone de Beauvoir

Recompense injury with
justice, and recompense
kindness with kindness.

Confucius

Saints were saints because they acted with loving kindness whether they felt like it or not.

Dan Millman

Since you get more joy out of giving joy to others, you should put a good deal of thought into the happiness that you are able to give.

Eleanor Roosevelt

301

Skip the religion and politics,
head straight to the compassion.
Everything else is a distraction.

Talib Kweli

Society tends to pit women against each other, but we need to treat each other with kindness and compliment one another instead. Because women's voices are the strongest when they're together.

Normani Kordei

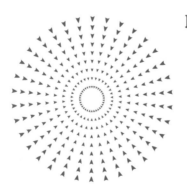

Teach me to feel another's woe,
To hide the fault I see,
That mercy I to others show,
That mercy show to me.

Alexander Pope

The first thing a kindness
deserves is acceptance,
the second, transmission.

George MacDonald

The most truly generous persons are
those who give silently without hope of
praise or reward.

Carol Ryrie Brink

The purpose of human life is to serve, and to show compassion and the will to help others.

Albert Schweitzer

The rule of friendship means there should be mutual sympathy between them, each supplying what the other lacks and trying to benefit the other, always using friendly and sincere words.

Marcus Tullius Cicero

The true greatness of a person, in my view, is evident in the way he or she treats those with whom courtesy and kindness are not required.

Joseph B. Wirthlin

There is no duty more obligatory than the repayment of kindness.

Cicero

There's no use doing a kindness if you do it a day too late.

Charles Kingsley

Three things in human life are important. The first is to be kind. The second is to be kind. And the third is to be kind.

Henry James

To be truly stylish, you have
to be kind and courteous.

Douglas Booth

To God be humble, to thy friend be kind,
And with thy neighbours gladly lend
   and borrow;
His chance tonight, it maybe thine
   tomorrow.

William Dunbar

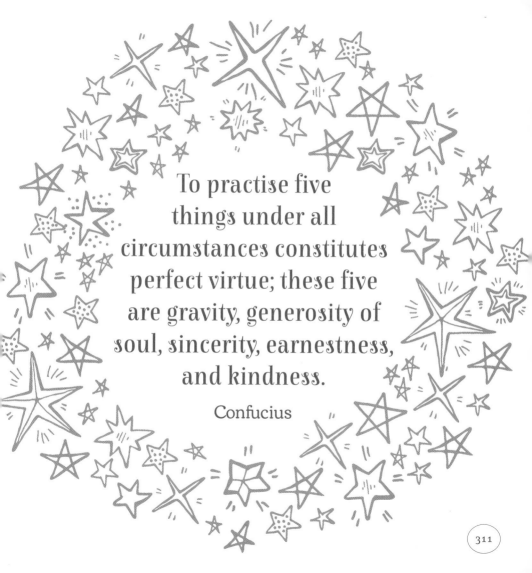

To practise five things under all circumstances constitutes perfect virtue; these five are gravity, generosity of soul, sincerity, earnestness, and kindness.

Confucius

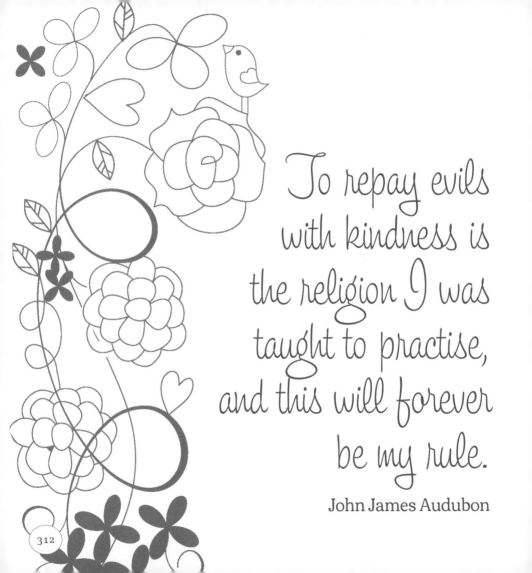

To repay evils
with kindness is
the religion I was
taught to practise,
and this will forever
be my rule.

John James Audubon

312

Try to exercise gentleness, kindness and humour, and you cannot go far wrong.

Sophie Winkleman

We are each made for goodness, love and compassion. Our lives are transformed as much as the world is when we live with these truths.

Desmond Tutu

We ought to be vigilantes for kindness and consideration.

Letitia Baldrige

What we all have in common is an appreciation of kindness and compassion; all the religions have this. We all lean towards love.

Richard Gere

When a thoughtless or unkind word is spoken, best tune out.

Ruth Bader Ginsburg

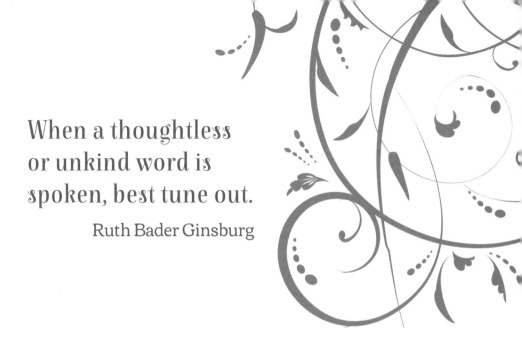

When you are young you take the kindness people show you as your right.

W. Somerset Maugham

You can give without loving, but
you cannot love without giving.

Robert Louis Stevenson

You cannot do a kindness too
soon, for you never know how
soon it will be too late.

Ralph Waldo Emerson

Your days are numbered.
Use them to throw open the
windows of your soul to the sun.
If you do not, the sun will
soon set, and you with it.

Marcus Aurelius

For beautiful eyes, look for the good in others; for beautiful lips, speak only words of kindness; and for poise, walk with the knowledge that you are never alone.

Audrey Hepburn

If you want others to be happy,
practise compassion. If you want to
be happy, practise compassion.

Dalai Lama

What do we live for, if it is not to make life
less difficult for each other?

George Eliot

Wherever there is a
human being, there
is an opportunity
for a kindness.

Lucius Seneca